The Lying Liar Called Racism

-A Love Letter-

Words by Giselle Fuerte
Art by Lesta Ginting

First paperback edition October 2020

ISBN 978-0-578-74618-0 (paperback)

Published by Real Life Bricks
www.reallifebricks.com

Book Formatting by Bluebobo

I dedicate this book to my children.
Believe no lies, my loves.

We're going to have a chat, you and I (and the grown-up reading this—hi there!).

I'm treating you like a big kid and giving you three big ideas that we'll braid together at the end.

These ideas might feel huge because they *are* huge, but I know you've got this. I have nothing but faith in you.

Off we go with
idea number one.

First, I'm going to ask you
to use your imagination. I
hear you've got a good one,
so this should be right up
your alley.

Look at this majestic mountain.
It represents you.

Let's think of some words to describe you as this
mountain. Mind if I throw some words out to get
you started?

How about *strong, confident, larger-than-life, beautiful,
powerful?*

I'm going to give you the nickname *Little Mountain*
to remind you of how strong and powerful you are.

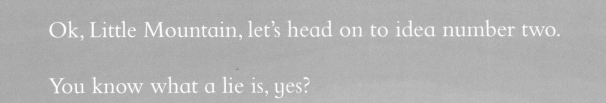

Ok, Little Mountain, let's head on to idea number two.

You know what a lie is, yes?

What if you know full well you are a mountain, but someone told you that you are a pile of spaghetti?

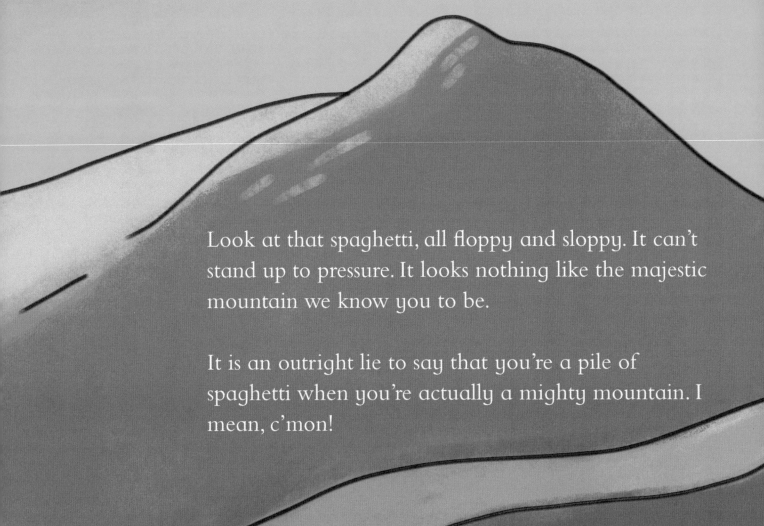

Look at that spaghetti, all floppy and sloppy. It can't stand up to pressure. It looks nothing like the majestic mountain we know you to be.

It is an outright lie to say that you're a pile of spaghetti when you're actually a mighty mountain. I mean, c'mon!

So far we've learned that you are Little Mountain and not a pile of spaghetti. Ready for idea number three?

Do you know much about your ancestors?

These are the people who came before you—
your parents' parents' parents and all the way
back down the line to your relatives who lived
a long, long time ago. Another way to say this
is your great-grandparents, and your great-
great-grandparents, and your great-great-great-
grandparents. You get the idea.

Let me tell you a bit about your ancestors. They
helped build cities and countries. They contributed
new ideas and wisdom, language and culture, art
and science, and so much more to help us live
more fulfilling lives. They survived deeply tragic
events and came out of them alive and well. They
continued moving forward to make a better life for
themselves, their children, and their communities.

You're here because your ancestors were resilient.

They were strong, creative, and powerful.
They were confident and larger than life.
Nothing could bring them down.

They were mountains. It makes sense that
you, Little Mountain, come from them.

Here's something that makes little sense, but I'll try to explain it just the same. This is where we introduce the villain of our story: The Lying Liar Called Racism.

There are people in this world who look at mountains and see spaghetti. It sounds like utter nonsense, but these people really exist.

They look at the color of a person's skin, the country a person comes from, the way they talk or the language they speak, and decide that the person is not at all a mountain.

They see that person as a small and insignificant pile of spaghetti. They think that person is not as good as they are.

The idea that someone isn't as good or as smart or as worthy because of their skin color, or because they come from a country where the sun shines bright much of the year, or from a place where an unfamiliar language is spoken, is called racism.

Racism is a lie. It is a bald-faced lie. It is a flat-out lie. It is a lying lie.

These people who look at mountains and see spaghetti—we call them racists—will sometimes use ugly words and may even disguise these words with a broad smile.

Or they might scowl, yell, and hiss ugly words to let The Lying Liar Called Racism into the world.

They might even get fancy and point to charts, graphs, and pictures to try to get mountains to believe that they are spaghetti.

Listen closely, Little Mountain. It doesn't matter if they stomp their feet and holler, or if they smile and purr softly as they try to convince you that you're spaghetti.

Always know that their words are lies.

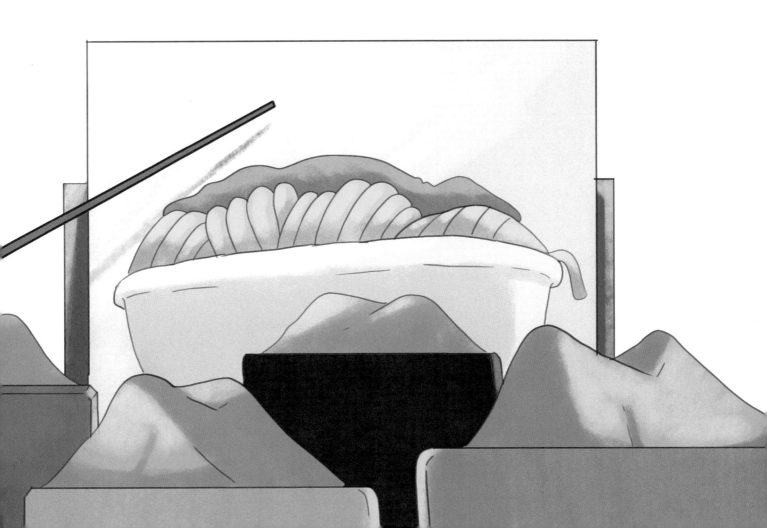

The day on which you should begin to believe their lies is Neverday of Nevuary.

(That's never—a NEVER EVER kind of never.)

Don't bother marking it on your calendar,
because the day to believe them will never come.

Just going to jump in here for a moment to talk about why some people spread The Lying Liar Called Racism around.

There are lots of ridiculous reasons, and listing all of them here will make this book taller than you, Little Mountain, so I'll focus on just one reason.

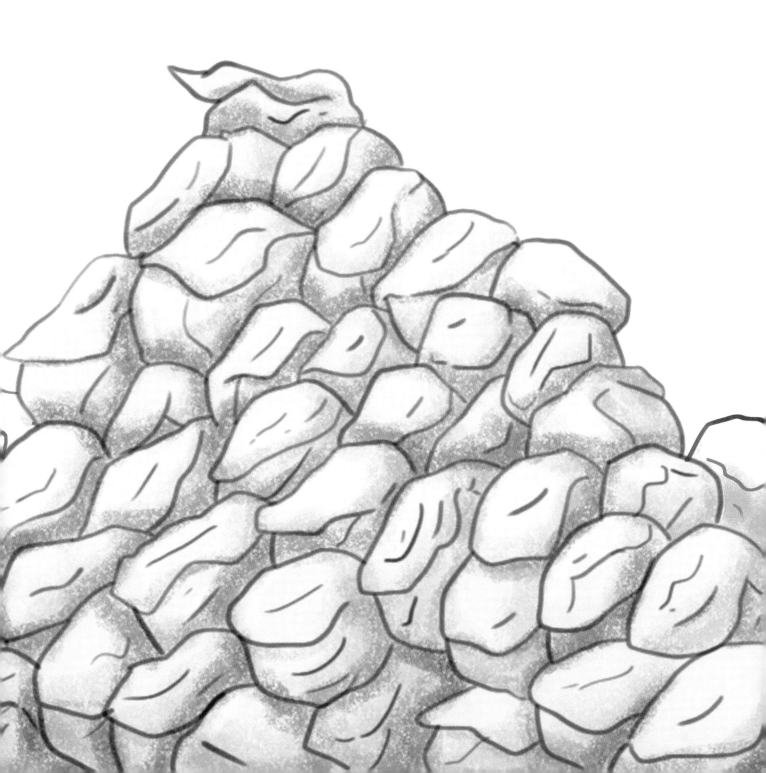

People who want you to believe that mountains are spaghetti are like the enemies in superhero books.

They want to rule the world, and one way to do that is to make mountains believe that they are tiny, weak, insignificant, and powerless.

If you think you're powerless, Little Mountain, you won't fight back. If you think you're powerless, Little Mountain, you might easily accept bad and unfair treatment.

You might even start to feel terrible about yourself and believe you deserve bad and unfair treatment.

Don't forget when you should start believing
The Lying Liar Called Racism:

Never, never, never, never, never…

So that you never start to believe
The Lying Liar Called Racism,
please always keep in mind the
three things you learned here: